Overcoming the Odds

Greg LeMond

Bill Gutman

RSVP

RAINTREE
STECK-VAUGHN
PUBLISHERS

The Steck-Vaughn Company

Austin, Texas

Published by Raintree Steck-Vaughn Publishers,
an imprint of Steck-Vaughn Company

Developed for Steck-Vaughn Company by
Visual Education Corporation, Princeton, New Jersey
Editor: Marilyn Miller
Photo Research: Marty Levick
Electronic Preparation: Cynthia C. Feldner, *Manager;* Fiona Torphy
Production Supervisor: Ellen Foos
Electronic Production: Lisa Evans-Skopas, *Manager;* Deirdre Sheean
Interior Design: Maxson Crandall

Raintree Steck-Vaughn Publishers staff
Editor: Kathy DeVico
Project Manager: Joyce Spicer

Photo Credits: **Cover:** © Lionel Cironneau/AP/Wide World Photos, Inc.;
4: © Lionel Cironneau/AP/Wide World Photos, Inc.; 8: © Vandystadt/ALLSPORT;
12: © Robert F. George; 14: © Robert F. George; 18: © Vandystadt/ALLSPORT;
21: © Graham Finlayson/*Sports Illustrated;* 23: © Gianni Ciaccia/SPORT VISION;
25: © REUTERS/Bettmann; 26: © Lane Stewart/*Sports Illustrated;*
30: © REUTERS/Bettmann/Archive Photos; 32: © AP/Wide World Photos, Inc.;
33: (top) © Lionel Cironneau/AP/Wide World Photos, Inc.; (**bottom**) © Vandystadt/ALLSPORT;
34: © Presse-Sports/*Sports Illustrated;* 35: © Vandystadt/ALLSPORT;
37: © Damian Strohmeyer/*Sports Illustrated;* 41: © Gary Newkirk/ALLSPORT;
43: © AP/Wide World Photos, Inc.

Library of Congress Cataloging-in-Publication Data
Gutman, Bill.
    Greg LeMond / Bill Gutman.
      p.   cm. — (Overcoming the odds)
    Includes bibliographical references (p. 46) and index.
    Summary: Describes the training, competitions, and triumph over near-fatal
injuries of the first American to win the Tour de France bicycle race.
    ISBN 0-8172-4130-2
    1. LeMond, Greg—Juvenile literature. 2. Cyclists—United States—Biography—
Juvenile literature.   3. Tour de France (Bicycle race)—Juvenile literature.
                clists.]   I. Title. II. Series.

97–15817
CIP
AC

Printed and bound in the United States
1 2 3 4 5 6 7 8 9 0 WZ 01 00 99 98 97

Table of contents

Chapter 1

An Incredible Victory

The Tour de France is not a race for the faint of heart. It is the world's most famous bicycle race and perhaps the most difficult sporting event in the world.

It is a race that takes 21 to 25 days to complete and covers 2,500 miles or more. The Tour is held in stages, with riders competing every single day until it ends.

Each competitor in the Tour de France is a member of a racing team. Teams, not individual riders, can qualify to compete in the race. During the racing season, the teams acquire points based on the finishing positions of their riders in the races leading up to the Tour de France. The teams with the highest points then can compete in the big race.

During the race each team member tries to win. However, teammates also help each other against competing teams. For example, if a rider from one team is in the lead, his teammates can fend off riders from other teams that might challenge him.

The rider with the best time for completing the specific distance for the stage is declared the winner

Greg rides down the Champs-Elysées on his way to winning the last stage of the 1989 Tour de France.

of the stage. As the race goes on, a leader emerges—the rider who has the best combined time for all the previous stages. The winner does not necessarily have to win any stage. He just has to have the fastest overall time for the entire course. Much of the race takes place in France and Belgium, but the course can take the riders into Spain, Italy, Germany, and Switzerland.

Each stage is different in distance. In addition, some stages of the race consist of all-out time trials, with each rider trying to complete the stage as fast as he can. Other stages consist of long, tortuous climbs into the thin air of the Alps and Pyrenees mountains. It is an exhausting experience. Repair vehicles for each team follow the cyclists. Many riders fail to finish. Others crash and cannot continue. The winner, however, becomes the toast of Europe and the cycling world.

No women can compete in the Tour de France. The best women cyclists have a separate race, the Tour de Femin. This race has fewer stages than the Tour de France. The stages also cover shorter distances than the stages of the men's race.

Before 1986 no American or non-European had ever won the Tour de France. But that year a wiry, 25-year-old American named Greg LeMond rose to the top of the cycling world by winning the Tour.

LeMond had been getting better and better. The first time he entered the Tour de France, in 1984, he finished third. A year later he placed second. So when he won in 1986, it was not really a surprise. Greg LeMond was that good.

In fact, many predicted Greg was on his way to becoming an all-time great. He was a cyclist people said would win the Tour de France many times. But in April 1987, before he could defend his title, Greg LeMond's career and life almost came to an abrupt end.

He was out hunting with his brother-in-law, when a shotgun accidentally discharged. Greg was hit all over his body with some 60 shotgun pellets. He almost bled to death. Speedy reaction by a police helicopter saved Greg's life. But most people thought he would never again be a world-class cyclist.

What many people didn't expect was the will of Greg LeMond. He refused to accept the fact that his career was over. Slowly he fought his way back. By 1988 he was racing again. A year later he returned to the Tour de France. Most experts thought it amazing he was even there. Almost no one thought he could win.

Yet Greg fought and fought. He finished first in two different stages. The final stage of the race was a 15-mile time trial that would end on the Champs-Elysées, a wide boulevard that runs through the center of Paris. Surprisingly Greg was in second place. But he was 50 seconds behind the leader, Laurent Fignon of France. It seemed unlikely that Greg could overcome a 50-second lead in a 15-mile time trial.

Greg is presented with the 1986 Tour de France trophy.

The riders began two minutes apart. They were riding against the clock, not each other. As Greg said later, "I went all out. I didn't think. I just rode."

The winds were cold and blustery. Greg hunched over in his seat and pedaled. He ignored his fatigue. He ignored the pain that is part of this cycling event. He just pedaled as fast as he possibly could, not letting up for a second. He crossed the finish line in 26 minutes 57 seconds. His average speed for the 15 miles was 34 miles per hour. That was the fastest ever for a Tour de France time trial.

Now Greg waited for Fignon to finish. The Frenchman was the last rider on the course. As Greg waited, he thought about one thing. He said later, "The last thing I wanted to do was race 21 days and 2,000 miles and lose the Tour de France by one or two seconds."

Finally, Fignon crossed the finish line. His time was 27 minutes 55 seconds. That was 58 seconds slower than Greg's time. Greg had won the Tour de France by 8 seconds. His victory was hailed as the greatest ever.

The cycling world marveled at Greg's amazing victory. But for Greg LeMond, overcoming the odds was something he had always done. Soon, however, he would have to try to do it against even more overwhelming odds.

Chapter 2

From skiing to Cycling

Believe it or not, America's greatest cyclist did not jump on a bike as soon as he could walk. Cycling wasn't even his first love. For a while it looked as if Greg would become an ace on the slopes, a great skier.

Gregory James LeMond was born in Lakewood, California, on June 26, 1961. His parents, Bertha and Robert LeMond, had two other children, both girls. Lakewood is in the southern part of Los Angeles County, and Greg spent his first seven years with his family near or on beaches.

Then, when he was seven years old, the family moved to Incline Village on the Nevada side of Lake Tahoe. Two years later they moved again, this time across a ridge of the Sierra Nevada Mountains to the Washoe Valley. The family settled between Carson City and Reno, Nevada. Mr. LeMond started a real estate business, and Greg found himself attracted to sports.

"I started skiing when I was about 8 years old," Greg said. "I used to ski a couple of times a week at Incline Village until I was about 13. I really liked moguls [a series of small jumps], and I flirted with the idea of getting into freestyle [skiing], but it was just so new at the time."

Greg was becoming a fine skier at an early age. When he was just 12, he enrolled in Wayne Wong's Freestyle Ski School in Carson City. Freestyle skiing involves flips, turns in the air, and other acrobatic tricks. Some call it hotdogging. That was the kind of skiing Greg liked. Oddly enough it was skiing that helped introduce Greg to cycling.

"I was up in Wistler, British Columbia [Canada], at a Wayne Wong freestyle camp," Greg recalled. "One of the coaches, Floyd Wilkie, told me that cycling was a good way to train for skiing. Everything really took off from there."

In the summer of 1975, Greg bought a Raleigh Grand Prix, a 10-speed bike, with money he saved from his paper route and mowing lawns.

"Once I got my bike, my dad decided that riding with me would be a good way for him to get back in shape. So he bought himself a racing bike, and we started riding together three or four times a week. At first, we rode for about an hour each time."

It didn't take long for the two to increase the distance. Before long they were pushing each other. Sometimes they rode for 60 miles or so, prompting Greg to say, "I was so tired I wanted to cry."

Greg still looked at cycling as a training tool. But in the winter of 1975–1976, there was very little snow for skiing. So Greg continued to cycle. That winter he

When Greg started cycling, he and his father rode together.

entered his first cycling race and won. The intense feeling of pleasure he had during the race changed his life forever.

"Before I got into cycling, I never did anything really competitive," he said. "Cycling kind of started a spark in my brain. It said, 'This is fun.'"

It also didn't hurt that Greg won the first 11 races he entered. Success was coming early, and it showed him that he had a real talent for the sport. At age 14½ Greg was in the intermediate age group. He asked for (and was given) permission to race with the juniors so that he could enter the Nevada City Junior Classic. Junior racers are usually between 16 and 19 years old.

"I placed second at Nevada City to Clark Natwick, who was second in the junior nationals that year. From that point on, I always raced against good guys."

Greg joined his first cycling club, the Nevada Wheelmen in Reno, and he continued to race as often as he could. By early 1977 he was so focused on his racing that he dropped out of Wooster High School in Reno. He would later receive his diploma through correspondence courses.

"I had become so fanatical about cycling that instead of listening to the teacher in school, I'd be writing my ideas on training . . . or whatever," he claims.

In his spare time, Greg read everything he could about cycling. He set training schedules and kept diaries. "Cycling was something I got totally crazy about," he said.

Greg continued to race and improve. His father entered cycling events for his age group, and the two drove in a van to all the northern California events. In 1977 Greg won the National Junior Road Championship. It was his biggest victory yet. Junior national road races usually are run in one day and are between 110 and 125 kilometers, or 68.4 to 77.7 miles long. So Greg was really beginning to race over long distances.

He was also setting goals for himself, and he wrote them down. As of 1977 he wanted to (1) win the World Junior Road Championship, (2) make the 1980 U.S. Olympic team and win a gold medal, (3) turn professional and race in Europe, (4) win the World Pro Road Championship, and (5) win the Tour de France by age 25.

Here's Greg in Princeton, New Jersey, at the trials for the National Junior Road Championship. The trials determine which juniors can compete in the big race.

If Greg achieved all his goals, he would be one of the greatest cyclists in the world. He wanted nothing less. In 1978 he began his climb toward the top.

He won 29 of 60 races that year. That's an amazing win rate. Now Greg wanted to step it up some more. In early 1979 he traveled to Europe for the first time. He raced and won in Switzerland, France, and Belgium.

"That was when I said, 'I'm as good as anybody here,' and decided that this is really going to be the sport for me," he said.

That summer Greg achieved the first of his goals. He won the World Junior Road Championship in Buenos Aires, Argentina. But it wasn't easy. Greg and Belgian rider Kenny De Maerteleire were head-to-head coming down the final stretch of the race. De Maerteleire tried to force Greg off the road, twice pushing him into a line of tire tracks on the edge of the course.

De Maerteleire crossed the finish line first. But the judges disqualified him for using illegal tactics, and Greg was declared the winner. The race gave Greg not only a major victory but also a hard lesson in the tactics of international racing.

Then came 1980, a year that became one of mixed emotions for Greg. In April he again traveled to Europe. This time he was part of the U.S. national cycling team. The team was there to compete in a series of pre-Olympic warm-up races, in which the cyclists try to compete in races that resemble the Olympics.

Greg showed his talent immediately. He won a 346-mile French race called the Circuit de la Sarthe. It featured both amateurs (cyclists who receive no money from their sport) and professional cyclists and was a stage race completed over several days. (Greg was still an amateur.) By winning, he became the first American—amateur or pro—to win a major stage race.

Then came the disappointment. The United States announced it would boycott the 1980 Olympic Games, which were to be held in Moscow in the Soviet Union. The boycott was called for political reasons, but the real losers were the athletes who had trained so hard for so long. Greg had already turned down several professional offers so he could compete in the Olympics. Now his quest for a gold medal was over.

Greg decided to accept an offer to join the French Renault team for the 1981 season. He was now a professional bike racer. In cycling all team members are professionals because they are paid by the team. A cyclist does not have to be a member of a team to race. But there are benefits to joining a team besides money. For example, the team provides riders with the team's bike to use as well as other equipment. Each team is sponsored by a company, such as the Renault Company, which manufactures cars.

That wasn't all that happened in 1981. Greg married Kathy Morris, a 19-year-old nursing student. He knew it wouldn't be an easy life for her. They would have to spend much time apart while he raced in Europe as well as America. In addition, American cyclists had not excelled in the sport, so it was possible that the couple would be financially stressed if Greg was outclassed by European cyclists.

"I was a complete nobody going off to do something that no one had heard of," he said. "She was pretty brave to marry me."

Chapter 3

Becoming a Champion

At 5 feet 10 inches tall and weighing just 158 pounds, the wiry LeMond was not a huge, powerful man. But he trained so hard that his legs were like pistons as they pumped the pedals during hard climbs and speedy time trials.

Racing in Europe against the world's best taught him something else. It isn't only physical strength and endurance that make a champion.

"I was confident," he explained, "but I learned that so many things go into making a rider succeed. A guy can have the physical qualities, but does he have the mental toughness to survive?"

Mental toughness enables a rider to keep going when he is dead tired—or when his lungs scream for more oxygen during a steep climb—or when his legs ache and feel lifeless after miles and miles of pedaling. The mentally tough rider digs down somewhere inside himself and keeps going.

Besides mental toughness, Greg had other qualities that make a great rider. It was calculated that he had the lung capacity one and a half times that of the

Greg's superior lung capacity gave him an advantage on steep mountain climbs. Here in the 1990 Tour de France, he rides ahead of Spain's Miguel Induráin in the 16th stage of the race.

average young man of his age. This was something he was born with, and it gave him an advantage over others, especially during steep climbs at high altitudes. The oxygen is thinner at high altitudes. That makes it more difficult to breathe.

During his first year in Europe, Greg won five races. He also finished fourth in a major stage race, the weeklong Dauphiné Libéré, in France. But his biggest victory came at home. He won the Coors Classic, held in the mountains of Colorado.

Greg's reputation continued to grow. By 1982 he was being coached by the captain of the Renault team, Bernard Hinault. Hinault had already won the Tour de France several times and was one of the best and toughest cyclists in the world. The French champion coached Greg on riding tactics and how to break the will of his opponents. Hinault knew all the tricks of the trade.

Greg learned fast. He was beginning to score big in major races. In the 170-mile World Pro Road Championship in Goodwood, England, he put on a dramatic last-minute sprint that brought him a silver medal—second place.

Later in the year, he captured first place in the 12-day, 837-mile Tour de l'Avenir in France. The way he won was even more impressive than the fact that he won. He blew away the field and won the race by a full ten minutes. That was a record for a major stage race.

In 1983 Greg realized another of his goals. He won the World Pro Road Championship. The 170-mile road race was held in Altenrhein, Switzerland. Each lap included a winding 600-foot climb, followed by another 2-mile climb up a 10 percent, or gently rising, grade. Greg later talked about how he felt during the race.

"Each time up," he said, "my lungs were on fire. And coming down, totally flat out, my eyes would water with the speed—tears streaming back along my temples and probably flying off, like driving a car in the rain.

"You're zooming 40 and 50 miles an hour downhill, and you're trying to see everything, straining to peek around corners when there's no way to see what's ahead. I don't like to take the lead. I try to pop in there in a second or third spot and then watch [the riders ahead]. If they crash, I can slow down in time. If they lose me on the downhill, I'll kill them on the uphill."

The mental toughness that he had learned from Hinault, combined with his own physical ability, was paying off. When 1983 ended, Greg was named the winner of the Super Prestige Pernod Trophy as the year's all-around cycling leader.

There was still one major race Greg had not yet entered. That was the Tour de France. By 1984 he was ready. The race would take place over 24 straight days and cover some 2,600 miles. Greg once compared the Tour de France to running one marathon a day for three weeks. A marathon is a grueling, 26-mile footrace. Greg's comparison shows just how difficult the Tour can be.

The race can also be dangerous. More than half of it is usually ridden on narrow mountain roads. Riders sometimes reach speeds up to 70 miles per hour on the downhills. Crashes can be fatal, even though the riders wear helmets, knee pads, and gloves. All the riders are at high risk, and only one man can win.

Shortly after the race started, Greg came down with bronchitis, which made breathing more difficult than usual. A lesser man would have quit. But he fought through the ailment. Yet after two weeks, he was still well in back of the leaders, some 15 minutes behind the overall leader.

It's time for the 1984 Tour de France, but for the moment Greg and his wife seem taken up with their infant son Geoffrey.

The bronchitis began to disappear, however, and when the cyclists reached the stiff climbs in the French Alps, Greg began to gain ground. He climbed like a demon, making up time on those ahead of him. When he crossed the finish line, he was in third place. That made Greg the first non-European to ever finish the Tour de France in the top three. Many people thought he would have won if he hadn't had bronchitis the first two weeks.

In 1985 Greg began to reap the financial rewards of being one of the world's best cyclists. He joined a new French-sponsored team, La Vie Claire, and he signed a four-year contract worth $1.4 million. In cycling, riders can choose not to renew their contracts with one team. They can try to get a better contract or conditions with another team. Or the team itself may decide not to renew a rider's contract.

The captain of Greg's new team was again Bernard Hinault. Hinault had already said that Greg LeMond was going to be the next great champion. But Hinault himself wanted to win another Tour de France. It would be a record-tying fifth win for Hinault.

That's when Greg began to learn more about the politics of international racing. Hinault's teammates, including Greg, were asked to help their captain win. This can be done in a number of ways.

Team riders can control the pace of the race. They go faster if the captain wants them to. They slow down if a slower pace will help. They can also allow the captain to "draft." That means riding directly in front of him to take the brunt of the head wind or air pressure, which could otherwise slow him down. Then, when the captain is ready, he can break away and sprint to the finish.

Greg rode a great race. He not only followed his team's instructions to help Hinault, but he showed the rest of the field what a powerful rider he had become. Hinault won a fifth Tour de France. But Greg LeMond surprised a lot of people by finishing second. He had also won the 21st stage of the race.

Once again Greg had made the best showing ever by an American. In the minds of many, Greg was already the favorite for next year's race.

Chapter 4

The Ultimate Prize

The 1986 Tour de France began on July 4. Hinault was entered in the race again, and Greg expected the Frenchman to help him the way he had helped Hinault the year before. But it didn't work out that way.

The huge crowds who came out to watch the cyclists were all rooting for Hinault to win a record sixth Tour. And when the riders reached the Pyrenees Mountains, it became apparent that Hinault had his own plan.

He suddenly broke away from Greg, who was left behind to deal with the group of riders pursuing him. By day's end Hinault had taken a 5-minute 25-second lead over Greg, who then ranked third in the overall standings. Hinault wanted to win the race.

Greg's face shows the real effort racing demands.

The next day Hinault broke away again. He was going all out for the victory. This was a very difficult stage of the Tour. It ended with a steep climb up a mountain. The climb finally caused Hinault to falter.

That gave Greg, who was always a superior climber, a chance to make up a lot of time. When the stage ended, Greg was within 46 seconds of Hinault's lead.

But the race wasn't over yet. Two days later Hinault made another breakaway, leading one of their La Vie Claire teammates to say that Hinault "was trying to crush Greg, to put him away."

Finally, Greg caught up to his teammate. He told Hinault that if they continued this kind of all-out competition, neither would win the race. By the end of the 17th stage, Greg took over the overall lead with an incredible surge on a dangerous downhill in the Alps. For the first time in his life, he wore the prestigious yellow jersey. This is always worn by the overall leader during the various stages of the race. Because yellow is a bright color, the spectators can always quickly pick out the leader.

Hinault made his last try to take the overall lead during the 20th stage. He broke away and then made up time when Greg took a fall and lost some 30 seconds. Hinault won the stage but still trailed his teammate by 2 minutes 18 seconds. At that point he told reporters that Greg would win.

During the last three stages of the race, Greg held the lead. But he continued to worry. For one thing, there were hundreds of thousands of fans watching, most of whom kept chanting Hinault's name.

"I'm scared someone's going to push me over," Greg admitted to a reporter. That's how fanatic the French fans were. But Greg finally pedaled on to Paris and took the final six laps up and down the Champs-Elysées. His winning time for the long race was 110 hours 35 minutes 19 seconds. He had triumphed over the runner-up, Hinault, by 3 minutes 10 seconds.

Greg was overjoyed to finally win the biggest race in cycling. But his sense of triumph was somewhat lessened by the unexpected tactics of Hinault. "I just wish he [Hinault] had said at the start it's each one for himself," Greg said. "If he had said that, I would have ridden a different race."

Greg LeMond had become the first American cyclist to win the Tour and had reached the top of the cycling world. Some predicted that, because he was so good, he might wind up winning the Tour more than anyone in history. But neither Greg nor any of his enthusiastic fans knew that the biggest battle of his life lay just ahead.

Greg takes a drink of water during the 19th stage of the Tour de France. His teammate Bernard Hinault is in the polka-dot shirt.

Chapter 5

A Terrible Accident

Greg joined a new team at the beginning of 1987, the Toshiba-Look team of France. As the Tour de France winner, he was also finally becoming a celebrity in America. Money was no longer a problem because of his $1 million contract and the commercial endorsements that came his way. He was free to concentrate on cycling and his growing family. He and Kathy already had two children, Geoffrey James and Scott. A third, Simone, would be born a few years later.

So everything seemed to be going well as 1987 began. Early in the year, however, Greg broke his wrist

Greg enjoys spending time with his family.

in a crash of several bikes during a race in Europe. He returned home to recover.

The wrist was just about healed in mid-April, and Greg planned to return to racing soon. Then, on April 20, he decided to go turkey hunting with his brother-in-law. The two men were hunting in a designated area on a ranch in Lincoln, California.

Without warning, Greg's brother-in-law's shotgun accidentally went off. Greg was hit, some 60 buckshot, or small shotgun pellets, entering his body. It was a terrible accident. The pellets entered his intestines, liver, kidney, diaphragm, and heart lining. They also broke two ribs and caused one of his lungs to collapse. He was bleeding and near death. In fact, he would lose nearly three-quarters of his body's blood supply.

Fortunately a police helicopter was on call. Greg was taken quickly to the Sacramento Trauma Center of the University of California, Davis Medical Center. This is a trauma center that specializes in gunshot wounds. The speedy response was the only thing that could save Greg's life.

At the hospital, doctors operated immediately. They removed about half of the pellets, leaving about 30 of them in Greg's body. Most of those remaining were in his back and legs, where doctors felt they wouldn't cause future problems. Several were also still lodged in the lining of his heart. Although these were too dangerous to remove, they might not cause trouble if left in Greg's body.

Even though his injuries were no longer life-threatening, recovery was slow and painful. And there was no guarantee that Greg would ever race again. But before he could even think about racing, Greg had to get over the terrible pain.

"I'd pace the bedroom and just cry and cry because it hurt so much," he admitted. "I never thought I'd be the type that needed painkillers. You think you're used to pain on your bike, but that's not pain. The suffering you feel on your bike is nothing compared to real pain.

"The shooting covered such a large part of my body, and I had such a long incision [from the surgery] that I didn't have any energy until five weeks after I got home."

Very few people thought Greg would ever again be a world-class cyclist. Yet by July, three months after the accident, Greg returned to training. He committed himself to getting back into racing shape. Greg had reached the top of the cycling world when he won the Tour de France in 1986. He wasn't ready to let it all slip away.

But nothing was easy. Within just a few weeks of getting back to training, Greg was rushed to the hospital again. The pain he was experiencing had nothing to do with his accident this time. He needed emergency surgery to remove his inflamed appendix.

By September 1987 Greg was ready to try racing again. But the first few times he went out, he noticed a big change in his physical ability.

"I couldn't sprint," he said. "As soon as I would try to go all out, I would go quickly into oxygen debt. I would be completely out of breath."

He also found he had lost some of his mental toughness. Once other riders broke away, he just did not have the stuff he needed to go get them. By 1988 he was on a new team, the PDM team of France. But he still wasn't racing well. He had yet another setback when he needed minor surgery for a shin infection.

Greg wasn't physically ready for the Tour de France in 1988. He felt, however, that all he needed to regain his form was time.

"No matter how dedicated you are," he explained, "how seriously you train, you need a certain period of time [to get back to top form]. It's impossible to go straight there."

At the start of 1989, Greg moved on to the ADR-Coors team, with sponsors in Belgium and the United States. He prepared to resume a full schedule of racing.

He began by competing in several one-day races and didn't do well at all. But his primary goal was to be ready for the Tour de France, which was to begin July 1. No one knew, however, if he would be ready.

In June Greg entered the Tour of Italy, a stage race not unlike the Tour de France. Once again he faltered. He especially struggled during mountain climbs, and when the race ended, he was 39th overall.

Then came more problems. Doctors in Italy discovered that Greg had a severe iron deficiency. The problem was not related to his accident, but it affected the oxygen supply to the working muscles. Once he was treated with medication, his performance improved. Now the Tour de France was less than a month away.

The 1989 Tour de France course was a difficult one. It went counterclockwise from Luxembourg around France. And there were four very difficult stages in the Alps. The way Greg had been struggling on recent climbs, it was hard to see him even competing.

But once the race started, Greg seemed to get a little something extra from somewhere deep inside him. He surprised everyone by finishing the first stage in fourth place. The Tour always seemed to bring out the best in him.

"I have a passion for this race I can't hide," he once said. Whatever that passion was, it was surely urging him on. When he won a time trial during the sixth stage, Greg became the overall leader. Right behind him, however, was two-time winner Laurent Fignon of France.

Greg and Laurent Fignon fight for the lead during the 1989 Tour de France.

The two riders continued to struggle for the lead. Fignon took over during the 11th stage of the race in the Pyrenees Mountains. For a while the two riders flip-flopped between first and second. Then Fignon took command once again in the 19th stage during more difficult climbs in very hot weather.

Now came the final stage, the crucial 15-mile time trial to end the race. Fignon had a 50-second lead over Greg and seemed to have won the race. But then Greg amazed the cycling world by setting a record—averaging 34 miles per hour during the time trial. Fignon couldn't catch him, and Greg won the race by 8 seconds. He had also won three separate stages of the race.

His amazing comeback made headlines everywhere. Once again he was being called the greatest cyclist in the world. He won several more races before the season ended, including the World Pro Road Championship in France.

It was a very tough race. With the rain coming down hard, Greg and Irish champion Sean Kelly raced neck and neck toward the finish line. Once again Greg showed his grit by coming up with just a little extra, enough to nudge ahead of Kelly and win the race.

After the race ended, an exhausted Greg said it was one of his favorite victories. Then he said something that would turn out to be prophetic. "I'll never do that again," he remarked. "I'll never feel that feeling again."

The Battle to
Stay on Top

The great 1989 season turned in by Greg LeMond had other awards besides his racing victories. *Sports Illustrated* named him Sportsman of the Year. ABC's "Wide World of Sports" picked Greg as Athlete of the Year. He also won the Amateur Athletics Federation World Trophy for 1989.

That wasn't all. His services were again in demand. In September 1989 he was given a three-year, $5.5 million contract with the Z team, which was based in France. At age 28 it looked as if there were many years of championship riding ahead of him.

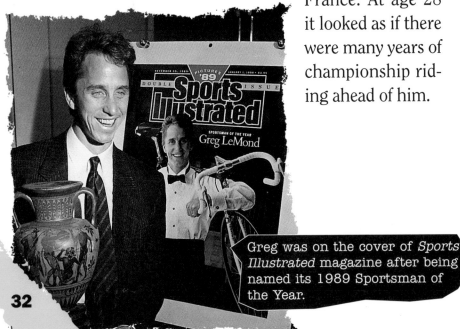

Greg was on the cover of *Sports Illustrated* magazine after being named its 1989 Sportsman of the Year.

On September 13, 1989, Greg announced his record three-year, $5.5 million contract with the French Z team.

In 1990 the situation appeared to be pretty much business as usual. Greg was riding well. He won several races early in the season, and then he won the Tour de France for a third time. He was still the only American and non-European to ever win it. Once again he was ABC's "Wide World of Sports" Athlete of the Year.

Greg raises his arms in victory after winning the 1990 Tour de France.

Greg would chat with reporters and fans for hours at a time. He didn't talk only about racing. He would talk about his love for ice cream and hamburgers and about hunting, fishing, and golfing. He thoroughly enjoyed being a world-class cyclist and media celebrity.

But just when it appeared that Greg had the cycling world by the tail, there was a slight falloff in his performance. It started in 1991. He won a couple of early races. And, as usual, in July he was the favorite to win another Tour de France. If he won, the victory would make three in a row.

Early in the race, he seemed on track for another victory. He wore the yellow jersey as the overall leader for four straight days. During the next stage, a thirsty LeMond was chasing a breakaway group on a climb. In the Tour de France, cyclists can at some stages get water from spectators at certain points along the course. Greg now made a mistake. He passed up a water stop to save time.

Greg has many interests besides racing, including fishing.

During that stage he lost the lead. That night he felt dehydrated and feverish. The next stage featured some difficult climbs in the Pyrenees. Greg began laboring during the climbs. He didn't look like the same rider who had won three Tours.

Greg pushed as hard as he could but crossed the finish line more than five minutes behind Miguel Induráin of Spain in the overall standings. He told reporters the race was "far from over." But that night doctors found his white blood cell count was twice as high as it should be, a sign that his body was fighting an infection. His feet were infected and full of open sores.

"It's not normal that I should be in such good condition before the race and so good through the first part of the Tour," Greg said, "and then suddenly have such a bad day." Antibiotics helped treat the infection, but on the next climb, Greg struggled so hard that he thought about quitting.

"My teammates were doing their best for me," he said. "I couldn't abandon them. Besides, people might think I was quitting because I wasn't winning."

So he continued with the same courage he had always shown. But courage wasn't enough. Induráin became the new champion, and Greg finished seventh.

"I've learned that I can accept defeat," Greg said afterward. "I came into the Tour thinking I couldn't lose, that anything but first would be a disaster. But, in a way, I feel relief. When you're bad, you appreciate when you're good, and this adds value to the victories I've had."

Then he added: "People like to see their heroes win, but they also like to see them be human. I'm not a bionic man."

But was something wrong? Earlier in the year, an exhausted Greg had dropped out of the Tour of Italy six days from the finish. And his performances didn't improve as the year wore on. He entered fewer races and wasn't in the top ten in any of them.

In May 1992 Greg entered the Tour Du Pont, billed as "America's Premier Cycling Event." The race was in its fourth year. In 1992 it was an 11-stage race of 1,006 miles. The route started in Wilmington, Delaware, and went through the Pocono and Blue Ridge mountains to Washington, D.C. There were 105 riders from 19 countries entered in the race.

Greg wanted to win very badly. Not only was it an important race, but he had not won a race in the

United States since 1985. He had trained very hard throughout the winter. Yet before the race began, he sounded unsure. "Anything can happen," he said. "I don't think I'll climb well. I'm really nervous."

It was apparent from the start that Greg was ready. He stayed up among the leaders for the first seven stages. Then, in the eighth stage, he took over the lead. Over the final three stages, he fought off all challengers.

The final stage of the race was a 14.7-mile time trial. Greg crossed the finish line to a huge roar from the American fans.

"I'm glad to have this one on my list at last," he said. "I've always been one to question how good I am. But I guess I perform best under tremendous pressure. Now, I'd say I've still got a couple of years left."

Greg grabs his lunch during the ninth stage of the 1992 Tour Du Pont.

That July a confident LeMond was back at the Tour de France. But suddenly things began to go badly. Once again Greg was having terrible problems with the climbs. He was far behind the leaders, and it appeared he had no chance of victory.

Then Greg did the unthinkable. He dropped out. He didn't race well for the rest of the season. At age 31 he wondered if he had passed his peak. "In every racer I know," said Greg's friend Kent Gordis, "the sign of aging is an inability to climb."

Greg himself was searching for answers. Just before the 1993 season started, he told the press he felt he was burned out in 1992. "The lifestyle is getting hard," he said, "all that traveling back and forth to Europe."

He sounded like a man getting ready to call it quits. But great athletes love to go out on top. He wanted a last victorious season in 1993.

But it didn't happen. There were, instead, more problems. He dropped out of three early stage races, and in June he announced that he would not compete in the Tour de France because of illness.

"My immune system is not functioning properly," he said. "I have had a hard time recovering for the past month. It's a combination of allergies with asthma-like attacks and a sore throat, as well as chronic fatigue."

So Greg returned to the United States with the hope of getting his strength back and racing again. But now that seemed questionable.

Chapter 7

Another Kind of Triumph

Once again Greg worked to regain his form. He hadn't won a race since the Tour Du Pont in 1992. Yet in each race he entered early in 1994, he seemed to run out of gas. He had just one top-ten finish when the Tour de France rolled around in July.

Maybe, just maybe, he could turn back the clock one more time. Again, however, Greg couldn't keep up with the leaders. During the sixth stage, while riding up a small hill, Greg just pulled over and stopped. He had completed 113 miles of the 168-mile stage. But he had had enough. He was done.

"I was accelerating," he said, "but it was one of those hills, one hill too many. I was killing myself to stay with the group, and I didn't have any juice left. I just ran out of juice."

Greg said the feeling wasn't new. "I haven't been able to recuperate in a race this year. I still have desire. I'm somebody who loves to compete. But an athlete who loves to compete wants to compete at the front. At least me." Now, Greg was almost in tears as he talked about his lack of endurance. "I don't want to race just to race," he said. "And I feel that's all I've done for the last two years. I had high motivation all winter, but I just keep getting knocked down—right down to the ground."

Greg's drop-off in performance seemed to be caused by more than just his body's aging. First he had blamed allergies. Then he thought he was carrying too much weight. He tried training harder. But he still tired much too quickly.

In August 1994 his doctors noticed that there was a big drop in his body's ability to carry oxygen. They removed some muscle tissue, which they examined to try to find the cause of the problem. The announcement shocked not only Greg but the entire cycling world.

Greg was suffering from a rare illness. It is called mitochondrial myopathy. It impairs the ability of proteins to reach the muscles. It had already caused a 30 percent drop in the oxygen-carrying capacity of the muscles in Greg's body. That explained why he had been tiring so easily during races.

The illness is not life-threatening, and doctors said it wouldn't interfere with his daily life. But because there was no cure or treatment, his days as a bicycle racer were over. Some doctors felt the illness might have been caused by the shotgun pellets that had remained in Greg's body since the 1987 hunting accident.

But the bottom line was the same. In December 1994 Greg made it official. He retired from racing.

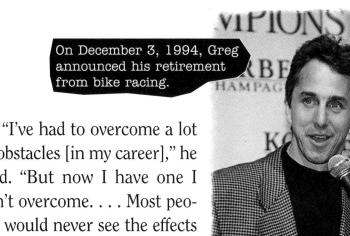

On December 3, 1994, Greg announced his retirement from bike racing.

"I've had to overcome a lot of obstacles [in my career]," he said. "But now I have one I can't overcome. . . . Most people would never see the effects of something like this [illness]. But cycling is so hard, even a cold keeps you from being world class."

While no one was happy about the final diagnosis, at least there was an answer. Greg, his coaches, and even the doctors had all been puzzled by his gradual decline as a racer since he had won his last Tour de France in 1990. Greg said, however, that his career really changed after his hunting accident in 1987.

"I break my career into two periods—before and after my hunting accident," he said. "In '85 and '86 I was always there for the victory, always in the race. Life was easy. I never suffered. But after the accident, something wasn't working right. I was lucky enough to win two Tours and the worlds [World Pro Road Championship] after that, but my career was a real struggle. I never felt the same strength that I felt in 1986."

Take away the near-tragic hunting accident and the onset of his illness, and Greg might have gone on to become the greatest cyclist in history. He certainly seemed to be on his way in 1986. That he came back after the accident was more than anyone could have predicted.

Greg retired from racing, but he wasn't ready to retire from life. His racing career had made him wealthy. He had a wife and three loving children. But he needed more.

"I'll need to find a challenge in the next year or two," he said. "Sports make you goal oriented, and I need the thrill of achieving something."

One of the things Greg did was return to his first love—skiing. Determined to stay active, he also took up mountain biking, a sport he fell in love with quickly. He soon began enjoying himself, once again trying hotdog skiing and even running some downhill courses.

He remained a spokesperson for a number of products. He also purchased a bagel bakery franchise and signed a deal to design cycling glasses for Bollé, a company that makes sunglasses and racing goggles. And he licensed a company to produce Greg LeMond racing bicycles.

After working so hard for so long, Greg LeMond is enjoying life and staying active in sports. He has also always been concerned with helping others less fortunate than himself. For example, he has become a national spokesperson for the Jimmie Huega Center. Jimmie Huega is a former Olympic skier who suffers

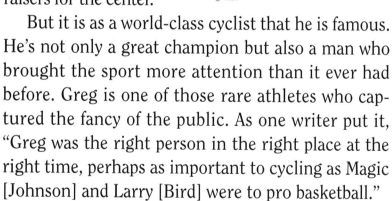

In September 1994 Greg shares a laugh with Rory McCarthy. They are helping to promote an eight-month, around-the-world cycling race for disabled athletes from 15 countries.

from multiple sclerosis. His center is dedicated to helping people who have that illness. Greg appears in Vail, Colorado, several times a year to race in both ski and bicycle fund-raisers for the center.

But it is as a world-class cyclist that he is famous. He's not only a great champion but also a man who brought the sport more attention than it ever had before. Greg is one of those rare athletes who captured the fancy of the public. As one writer put it, "Greg was the right person in the right place at the right time, perhaps as important to cycling as Magic [Johnson] and Larry [Bird] were to pro basketball."

Maybe the essence of Greg LeMond was best captured by Tim Maloney, a former U.S. cycling journalist. Even before Greg retired, Maloney wrote: "Greg has charisma. He's much appreciated in Europe as being a typical American—a relaxed, blue-eyed California dude who conquered their biggest sporting event and did it his way. There will never be another Greg LeMond."

Greg LeMond's
Career Highlights

1976	2nd, Nevada City Junior Classic, United States
1977	1st, National Junior Road Championship, United States
	1st, U.S. Junior World Trials, United States
	2nd, Tour of Fresno, United States
1978	2nd, National Junior Road Championship, United States
1979	1st, World Junior Road Championship, Argentina
	1st, National Junior Road Championship, United States
1980	1st, U.S. Olympic Trials Road Race, United States
	1st, Circuit de la Sarthe (stage race), France
1981	1st, Coors Classic (stage race), United States
1982	1st, Tour de l'Avenir (stage race), France
	2nd, World Pro Road Championship, Great Britain
1983	1st, World Pro Road Championship, Switzerland
	1st, Dauphiné Libéré (stage race), France
1984	3rd, Tour de France (stage race), France
1985	1st, Coors Classic (stage race), United States
	3rd, Biro d'Italia (stage race), Italy
	2nd, Tour de France (stage race), France
	2nd, World Pro Road Championship, Italy
1986	1st, Tour de France (stage race), France
	3rd, Tour of Switzerland (stage race), Switzerland
	2nd, Coors Classic (stage race), United States
1987	Injury and health problems
1988	Injury and health problems
1989	1st, Tour de France (stage race), France
	1st, World Pro Road Championship, France
1990	1st, Tour de France (stage race), France
1991	7th, Tour de France (stage race), France
1992	1st, Tour Du Pont (stage race), United States
1993	Health problems
1994	Health problems

Total Victories as a Professional: 43

Awards Won
by Greg LeMond

Year	Award
1983	Super Prestige Pernod Trophy (now World Cup)
1989	*Sports Illustrated*—Sportsman of the Year
1989	ABC's "Wide World of Sports"—Athlete of the Year
1989	Amateur Athletics Federation—World Trophy
1990	ABC's "Wide World of Sports"—Athlete of the Year
1991	Jesse Owens International Trophy Awards—World's Most Outstanding Athlete
1994	Korbel Lifetime Achievement Award

Racing Teams Represented
by Greg LeMond

Year	Team	Country
1976	Reno Wheelmen	United States
1977	Reno Wheelmen	United States
1978	Reno Wheelmen	United States
1979	Palo Alto-Avocet	United States
1980	Avocet and US Creteil	United States/France
1981	Renault-Elf-Gitane	France
1982	Renault-Elf-Gitane	France
1983	Renault-Elf-Gitane	France
1984	Renault-Elf-Gitane	France
1985	La Vie Claire	France
1986	La Vie Claire	France
1987	Toshiba-Look	France
1988	PDM	France
1989	ADR–Coors Light	Belgium/United States
1990	Z Team	France
1991	Z Team	France
1992	Z Team	France
1993	Gan	France
1994	Gan	France

Further Reading

Abt, Samuel. *LeMond: The Incredible Comeback of an American Hero*. New York: Random House, 1990.

Francis, John. *Bicycling*. Austin, TX: Raintree Steck-Vaughn, 1996.

Porter, A.P. *Greg LeMond*. Minneapolis: Lerner Publications, 1990.

Vande Plas, Rob. *The Bicycle Fitness Book*. San Francisco: Bicycle Books, 1989.

Index